Easy Rambles

Around
Patterdale & Ullswater

Vivienne Crow

Questa

ISBN 978-1-898808-35-0

Maps:
The maps accompanying the walks in this book are purely
diagrammatic, and are based on maps produced by Harvey Maps
(Licence No. 86413/2 © Harvey Map Services Ltd.)

Published by
Questa Publishing Limited
27 Camwood, Bamber Bridge,
Lancashire PR5 8LA

and printed by
Carnmor Print, 95/97 London Road, Preston,
Lancashire PR1 4BA

CONTENTS

NOTE

No attempt has been made to grade the walks in this book, as this is too subjective. Use the information about distance and height gain to calculate how long the walk will take.

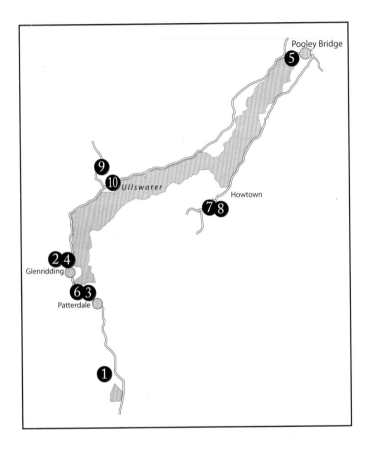

Pooley Bridge

Howtown

Ullswater

Glenridding

Patterdale

INTRODUCTION

Every valley in the Lake District is beautiful, every single one of its lakes is located in spectacular surroundings, and yet none can rival Ullswater for its sublime grace or its breath-taking grandeur. Ullswater is the second largest lake in the National Park, curling for more than seven wonderful miles through some of the best scenery – and the best walking country – that Cumbria has to offer. From the gently rolling hills and farmland around Pooley Bridge in the north to Glenridding, Patterdale and the very foot of the mighty Helvellyn range in the south, it carves its serpentine route.

The great Romantic poet William Wordsworth called its scenery "the happiest combination of beauty and grandeur", and devoted six pages of his Guide to it. The lakeshore is even said to have inspired his immortal lines, possibly the most famous lines in English poetry...

> *I wandered lonely as a cloud*
> *That floats on high o'er vales and hills,*
> *When all at once I saw a crowd,*
> *A host, of golden daffodils;*

The Lake District is essentially a massive volcanic dome fissured by tectonic forces and then sculpted by huge rivers of ice to create a spray of valleys and dividing mountain ranges radiating from a central hub – a bit like spokes from a wheel. One of these glaciers gouged out the deep, u-shaped valley that holds Ullswater. Even now, tens of thousands of years later, you can still see the deep scratch marks, or striations, left by the debris-laden glacier as it passed over this area. When the ice finally melted, the water filled the remaining hollow, forming the lake that exists today.

The changes in scenery as you travel up the lake are the result of changes in the underlying rock. The area around Pooley Bridge is surrounded by limestone and sandstone, but this quickly gives way to the Skiddaw slates as you head south and west. Laid down more than 450 million years ago and forming some of the oldest mountains in the world, these give us steep but smooth and rounded fells, usually covered in grass. Further south you come to the Borrowdale volcanics, a dramatic, craggy landscape that is the result of a cataclysmic volcanic episode that occurred about 450 million years ago.

The lake was probably named after a Norse settler, L'ulf, and it is just one of many instances of ancient peoples leaving their calling cards in the form of place names. The Celts, who crossed the Pennines from Yorkshire in about 300BC, introduced their Brythonic language – a predecessor of modern Welsh. Many of the names of the topographical features are Celtic in origin – 'glen' meaning valley, for example, appears throughout the district; and 'creic' becomes crag.

The Celtic kingdoms began to decline in the early seventh century and, before long, the Anglo-Saxons held power in much of lowland Cumbria. Their influence can be seen in place names ending in 'ton' - from the Anglian word 'tun' meaning farmstead. While the Germanic settlers farmed the valleys, the pastoralist Vikings began settling in the uplands of the Lake District towards the end of the ninth century. These weren't the raping, pillaging Danish raiders of modern mythology, but Norse settlers who had come from Norway via Ireland and the Isle of Man. Look at a map of Norway today and you will quickly discover why the Cumbrians call their hills and mountains fells – 'fjell' means mountain in Norwegian. The Norse word for waterfall is 'foss', which becomes 'force' in the Lake District, as in Aira Force; 'tjorn' becomes tarn; 'dalr' becomes dale; and 'bekkr' beck.

There is a good chance you will encounter some of the local wildlife on the walks in this book, especially if you are up with the sun or out for an evening stroll. High fell fauna include foxes, hares and stoats. Red deer can often be seen above the treeline, particularly on the eastern side of the lake where England's oldest native herd roam freely. The woods are home to badgers, roe deer, voles, shrews, occasional otters and the iconic red squirrel, sadly under threat from the incursion of the more dominant American greys.

The birds that make the fell-tops their home all year round include ravens, buzzards and peregrines, some of the most impressive of the UK's upland birds. You may even be lucky enough to catch a glimpse of England's last golden eagle as he roams the skies looking for a mate. Wheatears can be seen between March and October, as can ring ouzels, although their numbers are rapidly declining. Lower down, in the spring, you'll encounter migratory species such as redstart, pied flycatcher, wood warbler and tree pipit as well as the year-round residents, including chaffinch, green and great-spotted woodpeckers, nuthatch and sparrowhawk. Huge flocks of gulls can be seen on the lake itself, while mallard, coot, merganser and heron frequent the bays and the shallows. The rivers and becks are home to dippers, grey wagtails and common sandpipers.

The routes in this book, roughly in ascending order of difficulty, give a taste of the rich and varied landscape around Ullswater, while also introducing walkers to the area's flora and fauna as well as its fascinating history. Some walks keep to the valley floor, following idyllic farm and lakeshore paths where ramblers are dwarfed by the magnificent mountain scenery; some, like the lovely Glenridding Beck walk and the routes near Aira Force, head gently up into spectacular tributary valleys, flanked by steep-sided fells and home to impressive waterfalls; others climb easily accessible, low summits, such as Hallin Fell and Watermillock Common, for a bird's eye view of the lake. If you want to escape the crowds, try the route up lonely Fusedale. For a sense of Lake District history, both of the walks that drop in on the pretty little hamlet of Hartsop are fascinating, and the Pooley Bridge to Howtown route visits an area that is dotted with mysterious prehistoric remains and is crossed by the highest Roman road in the country. The latter is also the only route in the book that it isn't circular – it starts in Pooley Bridge and then returns to the village via the Ullswater Steamer, giving you a chance to enjoy these wonderful surroundings from yet another angle.

1

LOW HARTSOP
AND BROTHERS WATER

*This easy stroll is lovely on a calm, sunny morning when the fells are
perfectly reflected in Brothers Water, a tiny lake situated at the bottom of
the Kirkstone Pass, hemmed in on all sides by the mountains. As well as
a circuit of the lake, the route takes you up into the quaint hamlet of Low
Hartsop with its fascinating vernacular architecture. There is a little bit
of road walking at the start of the walk – and you will need to cross the
busy A592 twice – but otherwise the route uses good paths and tracks,
some of which are permissive routes.
There is next to no climbing and, as a special treat, it passes close to a
pub at almost exactly the half-way mark.*

> Start/Finish: Car park near Brothers Water on A592 (NY402133)
> Distance: 4.7km (2.9 miles)
> Height gain: 87m (284ft)

1. Leave the car park, turn right along the A592 and then, in a few
hundred metres, turn left along a minor road into Low Hartsop. Keep
straight ahead through the hamlet until you reach the parking area
at the far end.

> *This cluster of unspoilt stone cottages was once renowned
> for wool-spinning, Several homes, some of which date
> from the 17th century, still have their external spinning
> galleries. The best surviving examples are at Mireside and
> Thorn House, although there are others in the hamlet.
> Other interesting features on the buildings, 12 of which*

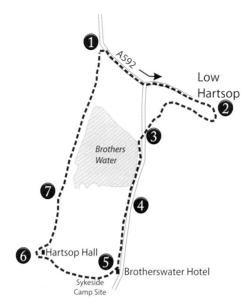

are listed, include stepped gables and circular chimneys.

It's hard to believe it now, but sleepy Hartsop was once buzzing with industrial activity. There were two lead mines in the area as well as a large slate quarry on Caudale Moor. The scant remains of Low Hartsop mine are still visible, about half-a-mile east of the hamlet, at the confluence of Hayeswater Gill and Pasture Beck. Stone piers and a wheel pit are all that remain of a huge water wheel that was constructed to drain the mine, which suffered badly from flooding.

2. Go through the kissing-gate and turn right – towards Pasture Beck. You quickly cross the beck and, immediately afterwards, turn right along a faint path. Once through the gate, the path becomes clearer as it follows the beck downstream. You soon join a path coming up

from a bridge on your right. This becomes a wider vehicle track. Keep straight ahead and, when it ends, a narrower, but clear path continues alongside a wall on your right.

3. Carefully cross the main road and go through the kissing-gate diagonally opposite. Turn left along the permissive path along the eastern shore of Brothers Water.

> *The views here are pretty impressive – the wooded slopes on the other side of the water lead up to Hartsop above How and the steep, bracken-covered ridge to the SW belongs to High Hartsop Dodd. The dark valley to the left of that is Caiston Glen.*

> *Brothers Water, regarded by some as one of the Lake District's smallest lakes and by others as one of its largest tarns, used to be called Broad Water. It was renamed in the 19th century after two brothers drowned there. William Wordsworth's sister Dorothy referred to it as "the glittering, lively lake".*

4. As you reach the southern end of the lake, the path climbs to the road. After a few more strides, go through a gap in the wall on your right to pick up another path running parallel with the road. Watch for deer on the flat, boggy area in the bottom of the valley.

5. Turn right along the Sykeside Campsite driveway. At a junction with another drive coming down from the pub, bear right again. Keep to the solid track, right through the middle of the campsite and then across some fields in the valley bottom.

6. When you reach Hartsop Hall, follow the track round to the left. It quickly splits and, when it does so, bear right. Keep close to the building as the track then swings right.

> *The first Hartsop Hall was built in the 12th century when Norman barons used the valley as a hunting forest. The*

*land passed to the Lowthers, still one of main landowners
in the whole of Cumbria, by marriage in the 15th century.
The area then became farmland and the hall was rebuilt.
Much of the current structure dates from the 16th century.
The hall remained Lowther family property until it was
bought by the National Trust in 1947.*

7. You are now heading back towards Brothers Water on a very popular track. This leads all the way back to the car park.

Red Squirrels

*Red squirrels can still be spotted in the woods near Brothers Water.
Cumbria is one of the last strongholds of these cute, fluffy-tailed
creatures. In most of the rest of England and Wales they have been
replaced by their grey cousins, introduced from North America in 1876.
Partly because greys breed rapidly, with two litters a year, and are better
able to survive a severe winter because of their extra body fat, they
out-compete the reds, particularly in lowland deciduous woodland.
They have been known to displace the native species completely within
seven years of arrival in a wood. Red squirrels are also more susceptible
to certain diseases, particularly the devastating squirrelpox virus, and
find it less easy to adapt when hedgerows and woodland are destroyed.*

*Several red squirrel reserves have been set up in Cumbria and the
Lake District. Conservationists hope that careful management
of woodland in these areas, including the installation of rope
bridges near roads for the squirrels' safety and the provision of
special food hoppers, will save the native species from extinction.*

2

KELDAS AND LANTY'S TARN

With an elevation of just 311m, Keldas provides surprisingly impressive views of Ullswater. This minor top, surrounded by giants, sits in a wonderful position that can be easily reached from Glenridding. The route described here also takes in pretty Lanty's Tarn – a great spot for a picnic - before dropping down into dramatic Grisedale. The paths are mostly clear and well signposted and, although they are a little steep in places, the climbs are all short-lived.

> Start/Finish: Main car park in Glenridding (NY386169)
> Distance: 4.4km (2.7 miles)
> Height gain: 183m (600ft)

1. From the entrance to the pay and display car park in Glenridding, turn right along the main road and then right again immediately after crossing Glenridding Beck. This is signposted Mires Beck and Helvellyn. A few metres after the asphalt ends, bear left at a fork – towards Lanty's Tarn and Helvellyn.

2. As you draw level with a garage door between two cottages on your right, go through the gap in the fence on your left. After the small gate, turn right and you quickly reach a constructed path, along which you bear left, heading uphill through the trees.

3. After the next kissing-gate, the path swings right and the views start to open out. To your right, you can see Glenridding Dodd and Heron Pike towering above the miners' cottages on the other side of the valley. With Birkhouse Moor straight ahead, you soon approach another small gate. Instead of going through this one, swing left,

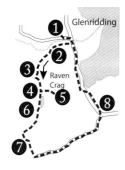

continuing uphill. The winding nature of this path means you get a new view with every turn – straight ahead now is Place Fell.

4. The path drops to a gate, beyond which you can see Lanty's Tarn. But before you head that way, cross the stile beside the gate just off to the left for a short climb on to Keldas for a lovely view of Ullswater. This is private land with just this one permissive path, so don't be tempted by any paths off to the left. At any point when you are faced with a choice, simply keep to the right and, eventually, you will clamber to the top of this pine-covered knoll.

> Keldas is known for its view of Ullswater, but there is plenty to see in other directions too. If you look to the SW, although the view up Grisedale is partly restricted by trees, you can see some impressive mountain scenery, including St Sunday Crag and the steep ridges leading on to Helvellyn's nearest neighbours, Nethermost Pike and Dollywaggon Pike.

5. Once you've rested and taken your photographs, you must retrace your steps to the gate near Lanty's Tarn. Go through the gate to access this lovely, calm stretch of water surrounded by trees.

> The tarn was named after Lancelot Dobson, whose family owned much of Grisedale in the 18th century. They lived in a large mansion near Grassthwaite Howe. The tarn was enlarged by the Marshall family, local benefactors who lived at Patterdale Hall. They fished here and also built themselves an ice house where they stored ice from the tarn - in many feet of sawdust and straw - for use in the summer.

6. Continue along the track beside the tarn and beyond. It descends to a fingerpost. Walk in the direction of Helvellyn for a few more metres

and then, when the path forks, bear left. Go through the large wooden gate and turn left, straight down the slope, badly eroded by a lethal combination of walkers' boots and water.

7. Go through the kissing-gate at a bend in a surfaced lane. Bear right along this lane (straight ahead) and cross Grisedale Beck via an old humpback bridge. Keep to the lane when it turns sharp left.

> When in spate, Grisedale Beck makes for a lively, if slightly manic companion as you both make your way down towards the lake. The grounds on the northern side of the beck belong to Patterdale Hall, built in 1796 by the 'King of Patterdale', one of the Mounsey dynasty. The first Mounsey to be granted the local hereditary title was John, who helped defeat a Scots raiding party on Stybarrow Crag.
>
> William Wordsworth's sister Dorothy strongly objected to Patterdale Hall, saying it was unsuitable for the valley. She particularly disliked the colour, which was subsequently changed. Today, the building belongs to Bolton School and is used as an outdoor education centre.

8. When you reach the main road, turn left to get back to Glenridding. There is a permissive path on the other side of the road, which soon heads through the trees. When it ends near a boathouse, you will need to cross back over to pick up the pedestrian walkway. And, when this too ends, you will have to cross the road again to walk on the pavement. Be careful when crossing – the A592 can be very busy at times.

3

PATTERDALE AND LOW HARTSOP

Constantly surrounded by beautiful mountain scenery, this is a lovely walk through the valley carved by Goldrill Beck and the many tributaries rushing down from Deepdale and from the slopes of Angletarn Pikes. The route never climbs any higher than 700ft above sea level, so there is relatively little ascent involved. It follows mostly clear and well waymarked tracks and paths from Patterdale to the historic hamlet of Low Hartsop, and then returns via woodland and paths beside the A592.

> Start/Finish: George Starkey Hut in Patterdale (NY394160)
> Distance: 8km (5 miles)
> Height gain: 180m (589ft)

1. Walk along the track to the left of the George Starkey Hut in Patterdale, towards Howtown and Boredale, soon crossing a wooden bridge over Goldrill Beck. Straight ahead is Place Fell, and the buildings tucked in at the bottom of its steep slopes belong to Side Farm. The track takes you right up to and through the farmyard. At a junction of paths, turn right, towards Hartsop, to pass the farmhouse on your right.

2. At the next set of buildings – about 250 metres beyond the farm – go through the gate and then keep straight ahead, along a surfaced lane. Go past some cottages and, when the lane bends to the right, turn left, towards Hartsop. Passing a series of pretty stone cottages and converted barns along the way, you eventually reach the farm at Crookabeck, which has a small flock of Angora goats.

> *Angora goats originate from Turkey and were first brought to Europe in the 16th century. Their long fleeces*

produce mohair, one of the softest types of wool in the world. Unlike sheep, which are shorn annually, goats are clipped twice a year. A large doe will produce between six and eight kilograms of fibre per year.

3. As soon as you pass an open-sided shed on your right, turn left through a gap in the stone wall. The path quickly crosses a narrow footbridge before winding its way round the back of a small outbuilding and then dropping down to a rough track, along which you turn left. Continue along this good, wide track, reaching the farm buildings at Beckstones close to where Deepdale Beck joins Goldrill Beck below.

4. Where you go through a gate to reach a track at a bend, bear left to head slightly uphill – towards Hartsop. Keep straight ahead when you encounter another track coming down from the left.

5. Just before you reach the bridge over Angletarn Beck, bear left up a faint path heading towards the beck. Ford it just a few yards upstream of the bridge. (If the water level is too high, you will need to use the bridge and then clamber your way up the bank.) Go through the small gate on the southern side of the beck to pick up a fairly clear path that roughly follows the wall on your right at first. Keep to the clearest path at all times. After an area of woodland, you will pass beneath a small crag and then through a gate. When the fence on your right ends, swing left along the vehicle track. This climbs briefly before dropping down into Low Hartsop.

6. When you reach the hamlet, turn right along the quiet lane. Having left the buildings behind, ignore one road turning on your right and then, when you reach a T-junction with the main road, turn right. In about 320 metres, turn left into the car park. Having crossed the bridge, go through the small gate straight ahead, ignoring the one on your left. As the National Trust sign indicates, this provides access to a permissive off-road route to Patterdale which runs parallel with the A592 through woodland.

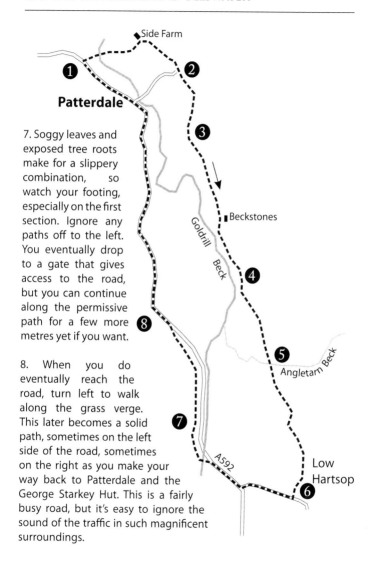

7. Soggy leaves and exposed tree roots make for a slippery combination, so watch your footing, especially on the first section. Ignore any paths off to the left. You eventually drop to a gate that gives access to the road, but you can continue along the permissive path for a few more metres yet if you want.

8. When you do eventually reach the road, turn left to walk along the grass verge. This later becomes a solid path, sometimes on the left side of the road, sometimes on the right as you make your way back to Patterdale and the George Starkey Hut. This is a fairly busy road, but it's easy to ignore the sound of the traffic in such magnificent surroundings.

Patterdale is said to be named after St Patrick. Local legend has it that, when his ship foundered on Duddon Sands, he walked across the mountains and ended up in this isolated valley. He is said to have baptised converts in St Patrick's Well nearby. The settlement was known as Patrichesdale in the 12th century and became Patricdale in the 13th century.

Like many parts of western Britain, Cumbria claims the patron saint of Ireland as her own son, but all that is known of his origins is that he was the son of a Roman tax collector at 'Banavem Tabernia' and was enslaved by Irish sea raiders. Banavem Tabernia has never been identified.

The church of St Patrick, just beyond the George Starkey Hut, was built by the acclaimed architect Anthony Salvin in 1853. The interior contains embroideries by Ann Macbeth, who lived and worked in Patterdale in the first half of the 20th century and belonged to the influential Glasgow School, which included Charles Rennie Mackintosh. The largest panel depicts 'The Good Shepherd', but there are smaller panels showing the Nativity and the score of Parry's music for Blake's Jerusalem.

4

GLENRIDDING BECK
AND GREENSIDE

*A gentle wander up Glenridding Beck is followed by a pleasant saunter
back down the other side – a relaxing way to spend a few hours, with
superb views of Ullswater towards the end of the walk. The walk passes
through some of the old workings of the Greenside mine, and a disused
leat provides a superb return route back to Glenridding, contouring the
northern slopes of Birkhouse Moor high above the beck.*

Start/Finish: Main car park in Glenridding (NY386169)
Distance: 6.3km (3.9 miles)
Height gain: 272m (892ft)

1. From the entrance to the pay and display car park in Glenridding,
turn right along the main road and then right again immediately
after crossing Glenridding Beck. This is signposted Mires Beck and
Helvellyn. A few metres after the asphalt ends, bear right at a fork to
continue alongside the beck – towards Gillside, Mires Beck, Greenside
and Helvellyn.

2. Turn left at a minor road and pick up the path running to the right of
the asphalt. In about 150 metres, you will reach two gates. Go through
the one on your right – towards Greenside Road. As you head along
the clear track, you can see the Glenridding Screes leading up to Heron
Pike on the other side of the valley. The slopes on your left belong to
Birkhouse Moor. When the track forks near a line of trees, bear right to
head down towards the beck. You will soon see a drystone wall that
comes to an abrupt end to the right of the track. Immediately after
this, bear right to cross Glenridding Beck via a wooden footbridge.

3. Once across, climb the steps to a kissing-gate and then bear left to follow a narrow trail that soon ascends the grassy slope to a gate in the wall above. Turn left along the rough vehicle track, continuing up the valley.

4. Eventually, you will pass the youth hostel and the various outdoor centres that occupy the old Greenside mine buildings.

> Lead mining at Greenside started in the 17th century, with Dutch adventurers driving the first level in the 1690s and then transporting the dressed ore to the Stoneycroft smelter near Keswick, 10 miles away. Serious development didn't begin until about 1822 when the Greenside Mining Company was formed. By 1849, there were 300 workers at Greenside, making it the largest lead mine in England. The mine operated until 1962, producing about 2,400,000 tons of lead ore and 2 million ounces of silver during its lifetime. After its closure, it was at one time leased to the Atomic Energy Authority who carried out non-nuclear explosions here to test seismic equipment.

> The mine is now part of a Scheduled Ancient Monument and is owned by the Lake District National Park. In 2002, the authority and its partners began work on making the site safe, a project that cost about £1 million. Spoil heaps were reshaped, new surface water drainage systems were put in place and repairs were carried out to dams, retaining walls and other structures. This work is expected to improve stability and reduce the risk of potential contamination from mine discharges.

5. Keep to the track as it swings sharp right and then sharp left just after the buildings. When it then forks, keep straight ahead – towards Red Tarn and Helvellyn. Once over the footbridge, turn left to begin the return route to Glenridding. This is slightly 'wilder' than the outward path, but still relatively straightforward. You will soon see a path off to

the left of this good track. This is actually the right of way, but ignore it for now; keep to the mostly level track that you are on.

> *This track is actually a disused leat, which would once have been used to carry water for the mining operations at Greenside. The mine was the first in Britain to use electrical winding and underground haulage, generating its own electricity by means of water turbines.*
>
> *The water was supplied by the damming of nearby tarns. One of them, in Keppel Cove, burst its banks in October 1927, bringing devastation to Glenridding below. None of the villagers was killed, but many buildings were destroyed. In fact, the promontory on which the modern steamer pier is situated is formed from the flood debris.*
>
> *The leat hugs the hillside at about the 330m contour and, as you stride out early on, you can look down into the cool, blue pools of Glenridding Beck, which flows through a rocky gorge at this point in its journey down to Ullswater. Further along, the track provides ever improving views of Glenridding and, on the other side of the lake, Place Fell.*

6. When you reach a wall cutting straight across the leat, bear left to head down a rocky path. This leads to a clearer track, along which you turn right. On reaching a gate, don't go through it; instead, bear right,

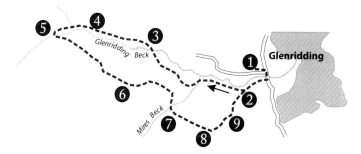

walking with the wall on your left for a few metres and then crossing Mires Beck.

7. Immediately after the steps leading away from the ford, leave this clear path by turning left along a very faint, easy-to-miss trail. This follows the line of the wall on your left and soon becomes more obvious on the ground. When you lose the trees on the left, the vista becomes more and more beautiful, culminating in a viewpoint that will stop you in your tracks as you crest a short, steep rise.

8. Be careful now because the paths up here are rather faint. Basically, you need to drop down to a kissing-gate which is about 200 metres to the NE of this knoll, avoiding the steep crag directly below. There are one or two narrow paths off to the left, but these cross very rough ground to reach the gate. It is better to continue ESE until you reach a boggy area with a tiny beck running through the middle of it. Bear left here, heading in the general direction of Glenridding (NE). Quickly cross the tiny beck and you will find yourself on a faint trail heading downhill. Keep right at a fork and then, just a few feet from the kissing-gate, the ground suddenly drops away. In dry weather, head to the right of this high ground to follow the wall on your right. In wet conditions, this can become almost impassable, so you will have to swing left and clamber down the rocks.

9. Once through the kissing-gate, head downhill on the clear path. It soon goes through another gate into a lightly wooded area - where there is a well-placed bench, should you want to savour the view of Ullswater for a little while longer. The path splits as you approach the bottom of the slope. Take either option; they both emerge on a wide track close to some cottages. Turn right along the track and you soon join the beckside route that you followed on your way out. This leads back to Glenridding.

5

POOLEY BRIDGE TO HOWTOWN

*This linear walk makes use of the delightful Ullswater Steamers, the
boats that shuttle up and down the lake between Pooley Bridge and
Glenridding, stopping off at Howtown along the way. There can't
be many routes in the Lakes that give walkers such fantastic views
for so little effort. The road and track climb on to the grassy, rolling
fells above Pooley Bridge at an easy angle - to a high point of 334m.
The mysterious moorland here is covered with Bronze Age remains,
including stone burial mounds and standing stones. Our route passes
an ancient stone circle, the origins of which have been lost in time. The
descent to Howtown, along a well-used bridleway with fantastic views
down the lake, is so gentle you'll hardly even notice you're losing height.
From Howtown, you get the Ullswater Steamer back to Pooley Bridge –
another chance to enjoy the beautiful surroundings. For timetables and
information on fares, contact Ullswater Steamers on 017684 82229 or
visit the website at www.ullswater-steamers.co.uk.*

Start: 'Steamer' pier in Pooley Bridge (NY467242)
Finish: 'Steamer' pier in Howtown (NY443199)
Distance: 8.9km (5.5 miles)
Height gain: 232m (761ft)

---

1. With your back to the 'steamer' pier in Pooley Bridge, turn right along
the road and cross the bridge over the River Eamont. Walk through the
village and then bear right at a small roundabout – towards Howtown
and Martindale. Go straight across at the next crossroads to stroll up
the quiet, tree-lined lane.

2. The asphalt ends at a gate. Go through this to gain access to a

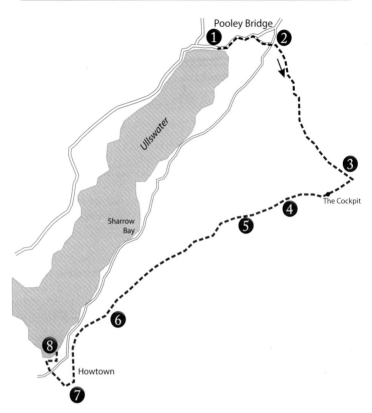

bridleway. Having climbed very gradually, leave the wide track when you reach a large cairn to the right of the route. Turn right here and walk across the open moorland on a constructed path.

3. Just before the path veers right to ford Elder Beck, you will see The Cockpit to the left of the path.

This stone circle, about 90ft in diameter, consists of

24

73 stones and a standing stone about 300 metres to the south-west. But what was it? A trading post? An observatory? Or maybe a religious site? Although it is a few thousand years old, it supposedly acquired its name in more recent history, when it was used for cock-fighting.

4. Reaching a large cairn 400 metres beyond The Cockpit, cross straight over a wide, grassy track that links up with High Street, the Roman road that crosses the high eastern fells.

Nearly 2,000 years ago, Roman soldiers marched along this very route on their way between the forts of Galava (Ambleside) and Brovacum (Brougham). It was the highest Roman road in the country and, even before the invading soldiers came along, it was probably used by the ancient Britons.

The Roman legions first entered the far north-west of England in about 71AD, when Petillius Cerialis began to crush the Brigantes, the Celtic people who dominated the region at the time. Agricola then managed to push north from Chester to Carlisle in 78AD and placed garrisons between the Solway Firth and the River Tyne. Although the Romans were soon clearly in charge and made allegiances with the Brigantes, the ancient Britons weren't truly quashed until about 140AD.

Cumbria and the Lake District is dotted with Roman military remains – forts, milecastles, marching camps, bath-houses and, of course, the magnificent Hadrian's Wall. This was built under the orders of the Emperor Hadrian after his visit to Britain in AD122. He wanted, according to his biographer, to "separate the Romans from the barbarians". It ran for 73 miles from Wallsend on the River Tyne to Bowness-on-Solway in Cumbria.

5. Immediately after fording Aik Beck, climb the narrower, right-hand path to a footpath sign next to a wall. Turn left – towards Howtown. Stretching ahead of you now is a mostly level track with magnificent views down Ullswater – the craggy, intimidating Helvellyn range forming a contrasting backdrop to the serene blue waters of the lake.

6. Walking with a drystone wall on your right, as you near Howtown you will reach a fork in the path. Bear left here. Don't worry when you see the buildings of Howtown and even the pier below you. Just keep going until you come to gate near a large house. Go through the gate on to a private driveway. Just before the gravel ends at another gate, turn left at a public bridleway sign. You soon cross a beck via a small stone bridge and climb to a signpost beside a concrete track.

7. Turn right along the track towards Howtown. About a quarter-of-a-mile later, you will reach the Martindale road. Continue straight across on to the private road to Waternook Farm. When this lane bends sharp left, go through the kissing-gate on your right to gain the lakeshore.

8. Howtown Pier is to the left immediately after you cross a small wooden bridge. There is a little shelter where you can sit and wait for the boat if you're early.

> *The Ullswater Navigation and Transit Company Limited started operating services on the lake in 1859, carrying mail, provisions and passengers. Two 19th century 'steamers' still operate – the Raven and the Lady of The Lake – although both were converted to diesel in the 1930s. A third boat – the Lady Dorothy – was brought over from Guernsey in 2001 and restored by a local boat builder, and Lady Wakefield joined the fleet in 2007.*

6

SILVER BAY AND SILVER HILL

Just over a mile north of Side Farm, the rocks above Silver Bay are a great place from which to gaze out over beautiful Ullswater. Steep crags plummet suddenly into the water below, while a grassy shore and shingle beach provide a perfect spot for a picnic. Having followed a clear, low-level track this far, the route returns via a slightly higher, parallel path, making a detour to the top of tiny Silver Hill (271m) for more of those wonderful views of the lake and the mountains. The lovely path then traverses the lower slopes of Birk Fell and Place Fell, passing some impressive disued quarry workings along the way.

> Start/Finish: George Starkey Hut in Patterdale (NY394160)
> Distance: 6.8km (4.2 miles)
> Height gain: 251m (824ft)

1. Walk along the track to the left of the George Starkey Hut in Patterdale, towards Howtown and Boredale, soon crossing a wooden bridge over Goldrill Beck. Straight ahead is Place Fell, and the buildings tucked in at the bottom of its steep slopes belong to Side Farm. The track takes you right up to and through the farmyard. At a junction of paths, turn left.

2. The vehicle-wide track quickly goes through a large gate, but do not be tempted by any of the other gates to the left of the track as you make your way out to Silver Bay. You get occasional glimpses of Ullswater and the Helvellyn range over the wall to your left. Up to your right are the surprisingly craggy slopes of Place Fell. The gently undulating track is straightforward, easily fording a few small becks as it heads north.

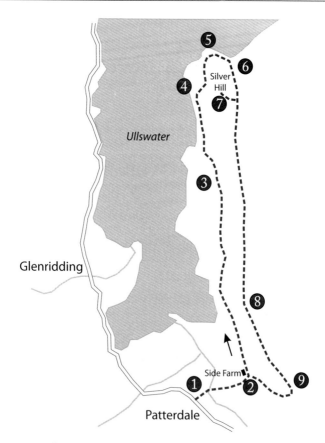

3. Eventually, the wall on your left swings away and you get a great view across the lake to Glencoyne Park. The path now drops slightly as it skirts the lakeside.

> Up to the right are the slopes of Silver Hill, thickly cloaked in juniper bushes. If you get a chance, squeeze one of

the berries and then sniff it. There's no mistaking which spirit this is used to flavour - gin. The Lake District used to be covered in huge forests of juniper, but much of it has gone now.

Its decline has been particularly marked over the last 50 years. Many old juniper bushes are not being naturally replaced owing to shading from other plants and grazing pressures from rabbits and livestock. Attempts are now being made in parts of the Lake District to replant areas with young juniper bushes. In Longsleddale a few years ago, climbers were brought in to plant the conifers on inaccessible crags where they would be safe from sheep. The berries provide an important food source for birds and animals such as field mice, squirrels and badgers. In the 17th century, the herbalist Nicholas Culpepper recommended the berries as a treatment for asthma and sciatica. He also claimed they could speed childbirth.

4. Before long, you reach a high point as the path swings slightly right – and you can see across to Gowbarrow. Leave the main path here by turning sharp left up on to the small promontory. The paths on the ground are unclear now as you explore this headland. Simply keep the water on your left and you shouldn't go wrong, but be aware that there are some steep drops from the crags.

Ullswater, the Lake District's second largest lake at more than 12kms long, has long inspired writers. Thomas Gray, in 1769, described it as "majestic in its calmness, clear and smooth as a blew mirror". Wordsworth said it was "perhaps, upon the whole, the happiest combination of beauty and grandeur which any of the Lakes affords". Praise indeed!

5. As you come round the NE side of the headland, you will pick up a path that drops down to the grassy foreshore of Silver Bay, a lovely spot for a picnic. Walk along the 'beach' for a few metres and then

head up the grassy path on your right. This soon crosses a beck and climbs towards a heap of slate.

6. You reach the main path close to a sprawling cairn. This marks the start of a pitched path heading south. Follow this, climbing at a moderate angle to a sylvan pass between Silver Hill on your right and Birk Fell on your left. As you approach the southern end of the pass, take the faint trail on your right, and, when this splits, bear right to climb quickly on to Silver Hill. A narrow path fights it way through the forest of juniper that covers the top, but it's worth the effort; there are great views across to the Helvellyn range and towards Kirkstone Pass.

7. Retrace your steps down to the pass and then turn right. You will soon see a gorgeous grassy path stretching out ahead of you. Follow it as it traverses the fellside, about 50 vertical metres above the track that you followed on the way out. There's only about 120m separating them, but the little bit of extra height gives you a surprisingly different perspective on the surroundings. It almost seems a shame to come down, so ignore any paths to the right that will take you back down to the track.

8. You pass a green Victorian bench, beyond which the path drops slightly, passing some dramatic old quarry workings on the way. Approaching the next set of workings, the path forks. Take either branch, although the one to the left is slightly easier.

9. Turn right along a wide, gravelly path above some stone cottages. Go through the large gate to gain access to the top of a lane. Turn right along the rough farm track. When you reach Side Farm, turn left between the farm buildings and retrace your steps to the George Starkey Hut.

7

FUSEDALE

Fusedale is a little-visited, green valley to the south of Howtown. There's a good chance it'll just be you, the sheep and the skylarks if you visit this peaceful dale mid-week. Having climbed slowly alongside Fusedale Beck, allowing yourself plenty of time to savour the tranquillity, you reach some ruined buildings just below Gowk Hill. The return route starts here, skirting the western edge of Brownthwaite Crag as you swap views of Fusedale for more dramatic views across Martindale.

Start/Finish: St Peter's Church in Martindale, 4.4 miles SW of
Pooley Bridge (NY435191)
Distance: 6.4km (4 miles)
Height gain: 323m (1,060ft)

---

1. Head up the wide lane to the right of St Peter's Church. As soon as the church wall ends, walk up the steep, grassy bank in front of you – ignoring the clear, wide track heading off to the right. A path swings left and then drops down to join a clearer track coming in from the right. Bearing left, you follow this lovely bridleway along the base of Steel Knotts until you reach a concrete track.

2. Turn right along the track – signposted Fusedale. Just before the cattle grid at the entrance to Cote Farm, turn right and cross a small stone bridge over Fusedale Beck. Once across, the narrow path heads up into green and pleasant Fusedale. You recross the beck in a short while via a small wooden footbridge.

3. The path heads away from the beck briefly and then veers right (SSE) on a sometimes muddy track. After yet another bridge – this

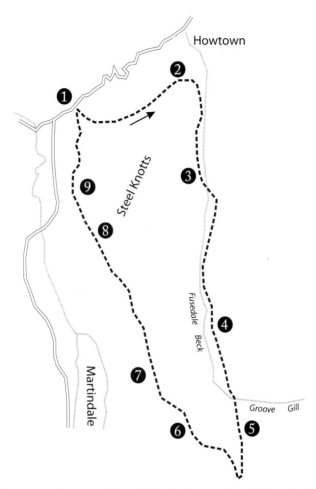

time over a tributary to the main beck – the way ahead is less obvious.
Follow the deep ruts created by tyre tracks until they turn a sharp left.
Now bear right (S) along a fainter path which, in 325 metres, rejoins

the main path close to the beck. If in any doubt, simply follow the beck upstream, staying fairly close to the valley bottom; and, eventually, the way ahead will become more obvious.

4. Beyond a ruined building with a bench outside it, the ascent steepens. The path splits as it makes its way along the northern bank of Groove Gill. Take either option; they both join up again to cross the gill. About 150 metres beyond Groove Gill, there will be a path off to the left. Ignore this.

5. After crossing some boggy ground, you reach the first of two ruined buildings. The path passes to the left of the first one, fords the beck and then passes to the right of the second, smaller building. Use the stepping stones to get through a damp gap in the wall and then follow the path as it heads away from the wall (WSW, veering NW) across boggy ground.

> *The fells above Martindale are home to England's oldest native herd of red deer, said to be the only herd that hasn't cross-bred with sika deer. The ancient deer forest itself is centred on The Nab, but the deer range all over these fells and into neighbouring Mardale and Kentmere.*
>
> *If you are here in the autumn, you may be lucky enough to hear an eerie noise, best described as a cross between the deep mooing of cows and the rumble of distant trail bikes. It is, in fact, the sound of the red deer rut. This deep roaring means the stags, who congregate in single-sex herds for much of the year, have gone their separate ways and are now gathering their individual harems for the mating season. The deep bellow of the stag performs two functions. Firstly, the loudest, most frequent roar wins the females. Secondly, it forms part of the posturing used by a male to achieve dominance over other stags. Another element of this is the antler fight, during which the animals lock antlers and attempt to push each other*

away. The strongest secures a harem for mating. Some stags could have as many as 40 hinds in their harem.

6. Keep to the main path at all times. It swings round to the western edge of Brownthwaite Crag, with steep ground dropping away into Martindale to the left. After the confines of Fusedale, this lovely path feels positively airy. You can see across the isolated valley to Beda Fell. Beyond that are layer upon layer of mountain ridges, each higher than the one before.

In the valley below, you should be able to make out a red-roofed building. Known as 'The Bungalow', this was the hunting lodge of the popular but eccentric 'Yellow' Earl of Lonsdale (Hugh Lowther), who lived from 1857 to 1944.

A celebrated horseman and yachtsman, he was also well-known in boxing circles where he initiated the presentation of the celebrated Lonsdale Belt to British champions. Because of his liking for yellow livery on his cars, horse boxes and coachmen, Hugh Lowther was dubbed the 'Yellow Earl', and his Lonsdale yellow was adopted by the Automobile Association when he became its president in 1907.

Among his many guests at The Bungalow and at Lowther Castle were Kaiser Wilhelm II, who visited in 1895 and 1902. On one occasion, knowing that the Kaiser liked to shoot rabbits, the Earl instructed his keepers to net as many as possible and conceal them in some nearby woodland. On approaching the trees with the Kaiser, he told his fellow huntsman that rabbits were often seen in the area. He then gave the word for the dogs to be sent into the woods and the keepers released the rabbits. Within seconds, hundreds of rabbits came running from the woods, providing the Kaiser with plenty of target practice.

7. Having bypassed the summit of Brownthwaite Crag, do not be tempted by any of the grassy paths heading uphill to the right. You go through a gap in a drystone wall and the path heads gently downhill.

8. About half-a-mile beyond the gap in the wall, with St Martin's Church almost directly below you, the path swings left and begins to descend more steeply. You now have two options. You can follow the path down to the church, turn right along the road and then follow the road round to the right, back to St Peter's Church. For a more pleasant alternative, avoiding the road, do not head down the steepening path; instead, bear right to pick up a faint, narrow path that runs just to the right of the old walled enclosure.

9. Keep the wall on your left at all times – don't be tempted by a path going through a small gate in a short while – and, eventually, after passing around the western end of a small crag, you come to a tiny, reedy tarn. Keep close to the wall as it swings sharp left here, and you soon reach St Peter's Church.

> *There are two churches in Martindale – the 'new' church of St Peter's, which is where the walk starts and finishes, and the tiny, isolated church of St Martin's, which you can see below you as you descend from Brownthwaite Crag. The latter, built in 1634, is lit by candle because it doesn't have any electricity. The enormous yew in the churchyard is said to be more than 1,000 years old. St Peter's was built in 1882 to replace the older church. A storm destroyed the roof of St Martin's on the very day that St Peter's was consecrated.*

8

HALLIN FELL

This great little walk is ideal on a sunny day, when the sun is glinting brilliantly off serene Ullswater. The route entails an easy stroll around the base of the fell and along the shores of the lake followed by a short climb to the top of Hallin Fell (388m) for superb views. If you can't face the climb to the top – which comes towards the end of the walk – it can be easily missed out.

Start/Finish: St Peter's Church in Martindale,
4.4 miles SW of Pooley Bridge (NY435191)
Distance: 5.3km (3.3 miles)
Height gain: 288m (943ft)

1. With your back to the church, turn right along the road – towards Pooley Bridge – and then bear left along a grassy path in about 120 metres. You walk parallel with the road for a short while, but then swing away from it to catch your first glimpse of beautiful Ullswater as you gently descend. Passing a kissing-gate on the right, the path swings left as it circles the base of Hallin Fell.

2. About 15 minutes into the walk, you find yourself strolling along a lovely path above the lake. Gradually losing height, you go through a kissing-gate to enter some woodland. Pick your way carefully across the rocks and protruding tree roots.

3. You will see a kissing-gate ahead of you when you approach the far end of the woods. About 50 metres before you reach the gate, take a narrow path heading uphill to the left. You soon climb steeply with a wall on your right.

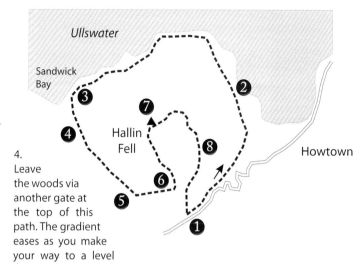

4. Leave the woods via another gate at the top of this path. The gradient eases as you make your way to a level section of path where you are greeted by a glorious vista of smooth, grassy fells and verdant valleys. The fell to your right, just appearing from behind the trees, is Place Fell. The next valley over is Martindale.

5. Leave the wall at a faint fork, bearing left along the clearer path, heading slightly uphill. The path soon levels off as you are joined by another wall to the right. You part company with this too at the next corner – as the wall turns sharp right, look to your left and you will see a multitude of green swathes heading up the fell. Take the path furthest left, rising in a NW direction. (Alternatively, if you don't fancy the climb to the top of Hallin Fell, turn right to drop back down to the church.)

6. Ignore any paths off; just keep heading straight uphill on the short turf. As you approach the top, the path swings right and you soon reach the surprisingly large 19th-century obelisk that marks the summit of this little fell – an opportunity to get the picnic basket out and relax while you enjoy the views.

The obelisk is said to be a monument to the first Lord Brougham, of Brougham Hall, near Penrith. He lived from 1778 to 1868 and was Lord Chancellor between 1830 and 1834. A lawyer and noted orator, he was a vocal opponent of the slave trade and backed educational reform.

7. Coming away from the top in an ENE direction, you soon drop into a dip. Ignore the faint path off to the right. You will start losing height more rapidly as you head down the NE side of the fell – soon passing a cairn up to your left. At the bottom of this initial descent, ignore a path to the left as the main path swings right (SSE). Bear right at an obvious fork (S). There are a multitude of paths criss-crossing the fell, but you're unlikely to get lost whichever one you pick – Hallin Fell stands isolated from all its neighbours, so the worst that can happen is that you'll end up wandering round in circles for a while. (A real possibility in mist!) The main trail gets wider and swings SSE again as it joins another path coming down from the right. At a dip between two small hillocks, bear right (S) as you join yet another path coming in from the left.

8. Ignore a faint track off to the left when you reach a prominent cairn; instead, choose the right-hand path (SSW). Always stick with the clearest option ahead as you shoot down the slope towards a wall corner. Now, turn left to reach the road opposite St Peter's Church.

9

WATERMILLOCK COMMON

Aira Force may not seem like the obvious place to go if you want to escape the crowds, but if you head SW, away from the waterfall and through delightful Glencoyne Park, you're unlikely to see many people at all. With great views of Ullswater for much of the time, this route uses a relatively little-walked footpath through the trees and bracken to gain the high ground. It climbs to a low ridge – 553m at its highest point – linking Swineside Knott with Common Fell on lonely Watermillock Common. If you've timed things right, lunch at The Royal in Dockray might be your next stop, before the final and busiest part of the walk – along Aira Beck and across the top of Aira Force.

Start/Finish: Small car park above Aira Force on the E side of A5091 (NY397205). This is 0.85 miles S of Dockray and is the second car park after the hamlet
Distance: 7.6km (4.7 miles)
Height gain: 399m (1,309ft)

---

1. From the car park, cross the road and climb the stile in the fence. A narrow, muddy path quickly joins another route coming in from the right. At a faint fork, keep right – along the clearer route. The lovely path climbs gently through the bracken and the trees, crossing several becks as they come tumbling down from Watermillock Common.

> *The wooded northern shores of Ullswater are said to have inspired William Wordsworth to write his most famous poem, Daffodils. Having walked through the woods with him on April 15, 1802, his sister Dorothy noted in her diary: "I never saw daffodils so beautiful, they grew among the mossy stones about and about them, some*

rested their heads upon these stones as on a pillow for weariness and the rest tossed and reeled and danced and seemed as if they verily laughed with the wind that blew upon them over the lake, they looked so gay ever glancing ever changing." Two years later, he used Dorothy's observations as the basis of that poem, the first line of which is probably one of the most famous lines in English poetry - 'I wandered lonely as a cloud...'

2. After crossing a stile in a wall and entering a thicker area of woodland, the climb gets a little steeper. Eventually, you reach a wall on the open fell. Cross the stile and turn right along a narrow path a few feet above the wall, but running parallel with it.

3. In about 150 metres, as the steep ground on your left gives way to a shallow col on the ridge, you will see a small knobble of high ground

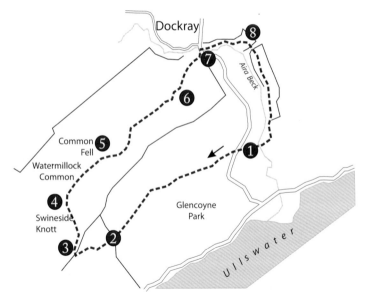

about 250 metres to the N. This is Swineside Knott, and it's your next target. To reach it, leave the path and make directly for it across rough, pathless ground.

4. Your next target is Common Fell, the small bump on the ridge about half-a-mile to the NE, but to get there you must first head to the small, rocky knoll just to the NNW, Swineside Knott's true summit. Be careful because the tussocky ground here hides some boggy pools. Beyond the rocks, surmounted by a tiny cairn, continue NNW to pick up a clear set of quad bike tracks, along which you turn right. The track heads N at first, veering NE, but it does weave about as it crosses some damp ground. It forks on the final approach to Common Fell. Bear left here and climb to the summit, marked by a small cairn.

5. Walk ESE to a large, solitary boulder. Then head SE down a steep, grassy slope to pick up the quad bike tracks again. Bear left, heading NE at first, as the track descends the grassy fell. When you reach a beck, Pounder Sike, cross it and turn left.

6. Walking with Pounder Sike on your left, you later cross another channel close to the edge of Dockray. Just after this, swing right – towards a small stone building. Pass to the right of this and go through a large gate on to a rough lane.

7. Turn left along the road and, when you draw level with The Royal on your left, turn sharp right, almost back on yourself, along a rough track – signposted Aira Force and Ulcat Row. The track eventually crosses a bridge and swings right towards Aira Force.

8. Before long, you enter woodland. At the first fork, bear left. At the next fork, which is just a few metres after the first one, bear right, downhill. Turn right to cross the stone, humpback bridge over the top of dramatic Aira Force and, having climbed the steps on the other side, turn left. Just after passing some steps down to your left, go through a small gate on your right. This provides access to a path leading into the woods and back up to the car park.

10

Swinburn's Park and Gowbarrow

This walk will take you only a few hours, but in that time you get to see a beautiful arboretum, one of the Lake District's most famous waterfalls, pretty cottages, isolated farmhouses, thick forest, open fells and a view that has to be one of the best in the eastern part of the National Park. Considering it never reaches the summit of any fell, there is a fair amount of ascent involved. Having said that, all the climbs are short, relatively easy and well spaced-out.

Start/Finish: National Trust pay and display car park beside
Aira Force at the junction of the A5091 and A592 (NY400200)
Distance: 12.6km (7.8 miles)
Height gain: 482m (1,581ft)

---

1. Go through the gap in the National Trust stone construction at the far end of the car park. Having gone through one metal gate and then a wooden gate, you reach a fork in the path. Surrounded by ancient yews and towering conifers, bear left away from the iron railings to slowly ascend, with the beck on your right.

> *William Wordsworth was a frequent visitor to the area, and wrote three poems about Aira Force, the most well known being The Somnambulist. This tells the local legend of two lovers who were parted by war. As the knight went off to fight, his sweetheart was left at home, worrying about him. Her anxiety led her to start sleepwalking along the edge of the steep Aira ravine. When the knight returned, he discovered her asleep*

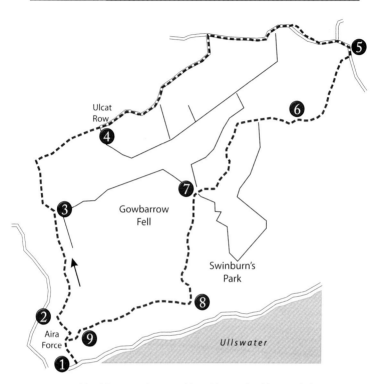

and in this precarious position. He touched her and she awoke, losing her balance and falling into the ravine. Needless to say, as in all good legends, the damsel died and the knight built himself a cell on the river bank to mourn his loss.

2. As you pass and ignore the first set of steps down to the right, you will see Aira Force through the trees. Go down the next set of steps to cross the bridge at the top of the waterfall and then turn left. There is quite a bit of clambering to be done – sometimes on slippery rocks - as you wend your way upstream with the beck on your left. After

43

following the beck for a while, you climb to a path junction where you bear left to continue in a generally northerly direction. At the next fork, keep right to stay on the higher path. The woods start to thin out after you pass through a gap in a wall and then disappear entirely.

3. Pass and ignore a faint path to your right heading on to Gowbarrow Fell and go through a gate. Just before the footbridge across Riddings Beck, take the track turning on your right – signposted Ulcat Row. A short, easy climb to a gate gives you access to open fellside. Beyond the gate, follow the muddy path at the base of the fells with a wall to your left. When the wall turns sharp left, continue straight ahead to pick up another wall on your left – don't be tempted off to the right.

4. You eventually reach Ulcat Row, where the grassy path gives way to a more solid track leading to a quiet road. Turn right along the road. At the next road junction, turn right again, continuing along the asphalt for another 1.1 miles.

5. Almost 300 metres after passing a turning to Dacre on your left, turn right through a kissing-gate – signposted Gowbarrow Fell and Aira Force. At a fork, bear left along the clearer route, heading slightly downhill to pass behind the old rectory. Ignore any routes off to the left after this.

6. Having gone through a kissing-gate at the top of the climb, walk with a drystone wall on your left for 100 metres and then cross a stile in a fence. Turn right here – towards a conifer plantation – and walk with the fence on your right. Once over the next stile, the path – muddy at first – skirts the edge of the trees for a short while before finding its way on to a ledge on the forested fellside.

7. You eventually leave the plantation via a stile in a fence. Quickly crossing a narrow footbridge, make your way up to and through a gate. The path bears slightly left, with the ruins of an old shooting hut on your right. About two-thirds of a mile beyond the shooting hut, you pass and ignore a faint turning to your right. Then, in another

five minutes, you're stopped in your tracks… Coming round the side of a crag, you are suddenly faced with one of the most magnificent panoramas in the eastern Lakes. The western expanse of Ullswater is revealed with the dark, craggy Helvellyn range in the background. Another 45 metres and you come to a perfectly placed bench – a chance to sit and admire.

8. The level path continues for a short while and then drops gently to a fence.

> As you descend, you will be able to see what looks like a medieval tower below. This is Lyulph's Tower and isn't as old as it looks; it was actually built as a shooting lodge in 1780.

9. Once through the gate, bear left at the next junction to descend through woodland to cross a bridge over Aira Beck. Climb the steps on the other side and bear left through a gap in some iron railings. It's now a five-minute woodland stroll back to the car park.

> Many of the trees in the arboretum here were planted by the Howard family of Greystoke. They were lords of the manor from the late Middle Ages until they sold the land to the National Trust in 1906. The fine specimens include a Douglas fir that is said to be the tallest tree in Cumbria, some ancient yews and a Chilean pine or 'Monkey Puzzle' tree. There are also two huge Sitka spruces on the eastern side of the beck. A much maligned species due to over-planting in British plantations during the 20th century, this pair dates back to 1846. The largest has a girth of more than six metres, placing it in the top seven largest Sitka spruces in the UK.

QUESTA
EASY RAMBLES SERIES OFFERS

DETAILED ROUTE DESCRIPTIONS
to 10 walks that are ideal for all the family,
young and old alike

plus

BACKGROUND INFORMATION
on things you will see along the way

Written by experienced and established outdoor
writers with an especial interest in and
knowledge of the areas visited

ISBN 978-1-898808-35-0

Front cover: Brothers Water
Back Cover: Hallin Fell
Published by
Questa Publishing Limited, Bamber Bridge,
Lancashire

9 781898 808350